Mixed Media Masterpieces

with

Jenny & Aaron

Mixed Media Masterpieces

with

Jenny & Aaron

Create Incredible Art Journals and Handmade
Mixed Media Treasures with Two Master Crafters

Jenny Heid & Aaron Nieradka

Founders of the blog
Everyday is a Holiday

PAGE STREET
PUBLISHING CO.

PAGE STREET
PUBLISHING CO.

First published in 2013 by
Page Street Publishing Co.
27 Congress Street, Suite 103
Salem, MA 01970
www.pagestreetpublishing.com

Distributed by Macmillan; sales in Canada by The Canadian Manda Group; distribution
in Canada by The Jaguar Book Group.

16   15   14   13   1   2   3   4   5

ISBN-13: 978-1-62414-028-0
ISBN-10: 1-62414-028-9

Library of Congress Control Number: 2013942559

Book design by Page Street Publishing Co.
Cover design by Jenny Heid & Aaron Nieradka
Photography by Jenny Heid & Aaron Nieradka

Printed and bound in China

Page Street is proud to be a member of 1% for the Planet. Members donate
1 percent of their sales to one or more of the over 1,500 environmental and
sustainability charities across the globe who participate in this program.

DEDICATION

This book, our first, is dedicated to our families... always in our corner, forever understanding of our less-than-practical ways of artistically navigating through life.

And also to our near and dear art community. To those selfless, hardworking souls who host art retreats and give instructors like us places to teach. And to all of the art and design lovers around the world who take classes with us, in person or online... the bloggers and blog readers... the Instagrammers and Pinterest addicts... without all of you, there is no us.

CONTENTS

FOR THE LOVE OF ART JOURNALING 78

Introduction

Before we pour the paint—before we pull out the brushes, the markers, the papers, the mediums, the scissors and the glitter—let the two of us first thank you for deciding to get creative with us. Nothing thrills us more than the give and take of making art with others. In developing the projects in this book we not only made the things that matter most to us but also considered what would strike a chord with you. From sculpting a fantastic faux cake from scratch, to making some fabulous artful jewelry, to getting out the detail brush and rendering a stylized portrait, you'll find countless new talents and discover skills you never knew you possessed. We find that mostly, the challenge of making art is deciding to do so. Every time we announce that we're teaching at an upcoming event we'll get a bunch of emails from friends asking if we think they'd fare well in the class, or if we think it would be "worth it" for them to attend. And our answer, unconditionally, is always "Absolutely yes." Because we know that none of this is beyond you and you've got nothing to lose and everything to gain.

This book is put together in such a way that you're not just learning techniques, but you're also making fully realized, totally completed pieces of art. Every single bit of work you see in the book is detailed in a step-by-step fashion. So, whether you like it or not—scared or not scared—you're going to be making some works of art . . . and they're going to be masterpieces!

Now, let's get down to the business at hand. The two of us have been creative partners in artful crime for our entire adult lives. We've made our way in the world solely by making art in some fashion or another. Though there have been many tangents and tributaries in our unified career, what we have been for more than a decade falls under the name Everyday is a Holiday. This name not only hints at our visual style, but it also is our career philosophy. Every day making art—every day living creatively and on your own terms—is a holiday. And specifically, what this entails is our illustrating and design work, our line of art prints and original hand-painted signs and home decor, our kits, our teaching, our online shop and our decorating. And at the center of everything, the catchall wherein we share everything from art journaling tutorials to healthy and yummy recipes, is our blog. This is where you'll find us in our element, and where we're always available. And this book you're holding represents where we're at creatively at this very moment. The projects and skills we'd love to share with you most are displayed on these pages. And creatively speaking, we hope that you'll be right on the same page as us!

In making mixed-media art the creative scenery is ever changing. Your list of special ingredients grows and grows, and the palette in your hand offers unlimited colors and textures. What's constant is what you bring to it. For the two of us, our likes, our loves and our faves are always front and center in any art we make. The cupcakes and cakes, the bunnies, the shelves full of vintage bottlebrush trees, tiny cardboard Christmas houses, toy pianos, glittery things, pink and aqua things . . . when we make art all of these are on the tips of our tongues—or tips of our brushes, you could say. This is what Everyday is a Holiday means to us and we wouldn't have it any other way.

Working in mixed media offers so many more opportunities to put a bit of yourself into your art. You don't need to possess expert talent for rendering with a brush. You don't need to be well versed in art history or know the ins and outs of perspective, light and shadow. Mostly, you just have to absolutely love stuff. And by stuff we mean color, collections, supplies, tools, papers, textures, ephemeral bits and pieces. The stuff you'd surround yourself with in a perfect world. As far as making art goes, doesn't that sound like an easy prerequisite?

In our art journaling we like to sample the best of both worlds. We love the clean, papery layers and careful composition of scrapbooking, and we love the messy, painty, hands-on approach of mixed media artwork. We hope that you can find your own happy combination of these two worlds when following along with us in these pages. Let your bins full of treasured embellishments live side by side on the page with your paints and mediums. What matters most in the end is that the artwork is undeniably yours.

Whatever your skill level, we know there's something here to spark your creative fire. And for those who are just beginning to venture into this colorful land of making, painting, cutting, pasting, sculpting and creating . . . oh boy, are we excited to extend our paint-covered hands to be your glittery guides.

CHAPTER 1

Painting, Making, Sculpting and Escaping into Mixed Media

As artists our career together has been of the make-it-up-as-you-go variety. But there is one thing that has always been certain: We are always at our absolute happiest when we're doing the things that we're good at. And knowing this, we try like heck to be good at a lot of things!

And in art, being "good" is totally relative. When we say good, we more or less mean interested, or inspired. When getting creative, variety is essential. For us that's what mixed media is all about. In putting together these projects—with bits of sculpture, some jewelry making, lots of painting, drawing, assembling, cutting and even making some faux sweets—the one constant is that we loved the creative process.

The only way to unearth your undiscovered talents is to try something new. We don't think it's lofty to say that we think you can find yourself through the artistic process. And we've got all the confidence in the world that you'll not only make some great art in following along with these projects, but you'll also make some great discoveries about yourself and how much talent you've yet to realize. Happiness truly does come with doing the things that you are good at—and doing them often. So if your creative curiosity brought you here, you're halfway there. The rest of the way is in the painting, the making, the sculpting and the escaping into mixed media.

CELEBRATE EVERYDAY

We think this project embodies the spirit of its title, both in subject matter (cupcakes!) and in the celebratory light it shines on so many of your creative skill sets. A lot of simple steps and mediums make up this fabulous piece of wall art.

There's painting and stamping, scrapbooking and assemblage, and even some faux wood graining. With so much to do and so many fun elements to play with, we're confident that you'll happily lose yourself in this mixed media party, and in the end you'll have an amazing work of art to display in your home.

SUPPLIES

12" x 16"/30.5 x 40.6 cm canvas board

Grain striping comb

Circular paint spouncer

Patterned paper

Recipe book page

Seam binding or ribbon

¾"/1.9 cm flat brush

#8 round brush

Hole punch

Scissors

Pencil

Ruler

Tracing paper

All-purpose glue

Decoupage medium

Pom-pom trim

Flag cupcake picks

Acrylic gel medium

Acrylic molding paste

Chipboard/game letters

Cupcake image template (page 169)

Acrylic paint

* cream
* pale pink
* chocolate
* white
* mocha
* burnt umber

DIRECTIONS

1. Basecoat your canvas board with cream paint. You may need two coats for full coverage. When the paint is dry, measure 4½"/11.4 cm up from the bottom edge of your canvas and draw a pencil line horizontally dividing the canvas. This will be your horizon/table line.

2. Use a circular paint spouncer to create your polka-dot background. To give your polka dots a faded or distressed effect, use a paintbrush to unevenly apply the paint to the spouncer. Stamp on your polka dots one row at a time starting from the top left corner and working across, staggering each row of dots. When you reach the horizon line, hold a piece of scrap paper flush along the horizon line as a blocker so that the painted polka dot only appears above the horizon line. Let dry.

3. To further fade and distress the polka dots, apply a wash of the background cream color over them. Mix one part cream paint with two parts water, brush over the polka dots and blot to the desired effect.

4. To create the faux wood grain, mix one part mocha paint with one part gel medium. Mix enough to apply an even coat to the bottom portion of the canvas. Use the ³/₄"/1.9 cm flat brush to evenly coat the table with your mocha/gel medium mix. Then, while the mixture is still wet, drag the graining comb horizontally with the smaller teeth of the comb at the horizon line. Drag all the way across the canvas and then repeat this motion on the remaining table area below. Let dry completely, about 10-15 minutes. A blow dryer helps to speed things along.

5. Use a photocopier to resize the cupcake image template to best fit your canvas. Ours is about 9"/22.9 cm wide. Then lay tracing paper over the image and trace the lines with a pencil. Press hard to ensure the lines transfer.

6. Flip the tracing paper and transfer the image onto patterned paper by rubbing with a smooth, blunt object. We use the back end of a Sharpie marker. Be sure to rub hard and thoroughly for an even transfer.

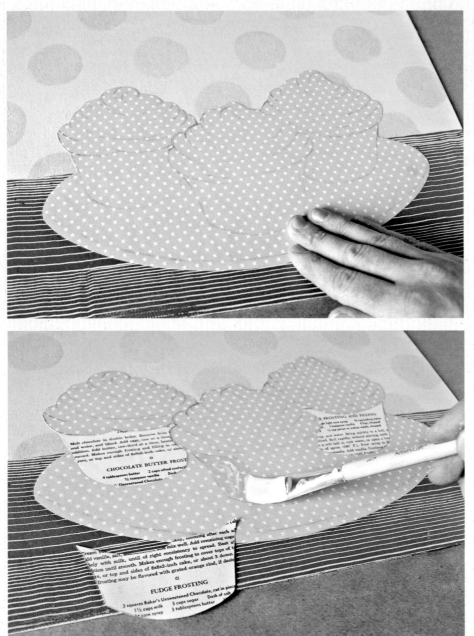

7. Cut out the transferred image and position it on your canvas so that the horizon line intersects the image where the cupcakes meet the uppermost edge of the plate. Adhere it to your canvas with decoupage medium, making sure to smooth out any bubbles. Let dry for about 5 minutes.

8. Use the same tracing paper to rub the shapes of the cupcake bottoms onto a recipe book page. Then cut out the cupcake bottoms and adhere them to your image with decoupage medium. Let dry for about 5 minutes.

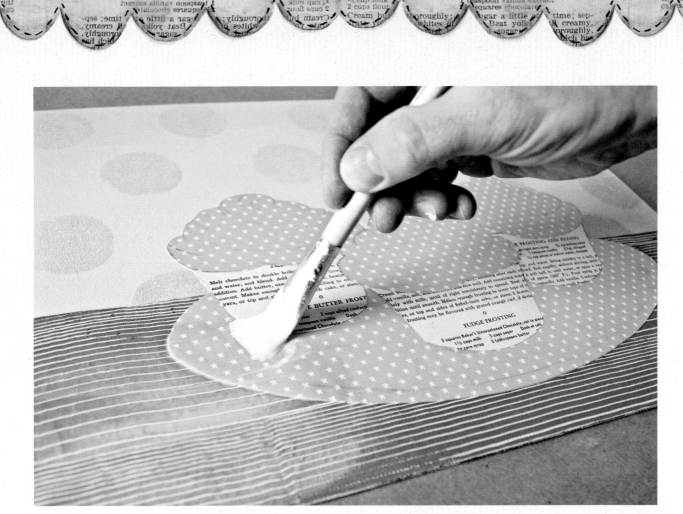

9. Apply a topcoat of decoupage medium over the entire canvas. Let dry for about 5 minutes.

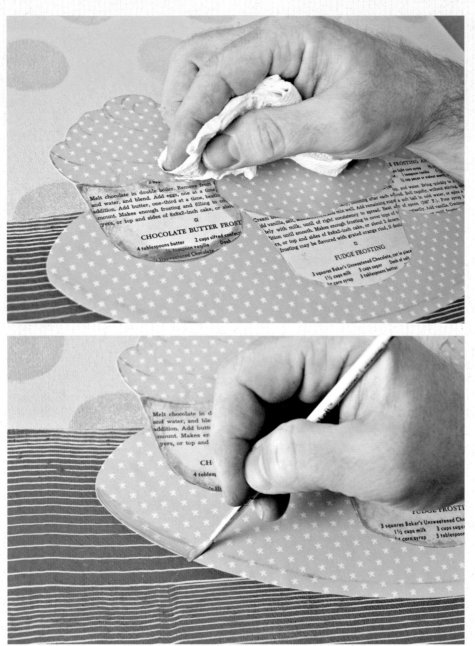

10. Mix one part burnt umber with two parts water, then apply the wash to the edges of each cupcake bottom and blot with a paper towel to the desired effect.

11. With a #8 round brush, apply a smooth line of the wash along the rim of the plate.

Melt chocolate in double boiler. Remove from and water, and blend. Add eggs, one at a time addition. Add butter, one-third at a time, beatin mount. Makes enough frosting and filling to co yers, or top and sides of 8x8x2-inch cake, or abou

CHOCOLATE BUTTER FROST
4 tablespoons butter   2 cups sifted confecti
½ teaspoon vanilla   Dash
unsweetened Chocolate

Cream bu
dd vanilla, salt, and mix well. Add remaining suga
tely with milk, until of right consistency to spread. Beat af
ition until smooth. Makes enough frosting to cover tops of t
rs, or top and sides of 8x8x2-inch cake, or about 2 dozen
frosting may be flavored with grated orange rind, if desir

E FROSTING AND FILLING
on light corn syrup   ⅔ cup boiling water
1 teaspoon vanilla   6 figs, chopped
½ cup pecan or walnut meats, chopped
up, and water. Bring quickly to a boil,
Boil rapidly, without stirring, until
a soft ball in cold water, or spins a long
of spoon (240° F.). Pour syrup in
antly. Add vanilla. Continue

12. Apply and blot the wash in the same fashion around the cupcakes, giving them an antique glow. Then do the same to the edges and corners of the entire canvas.

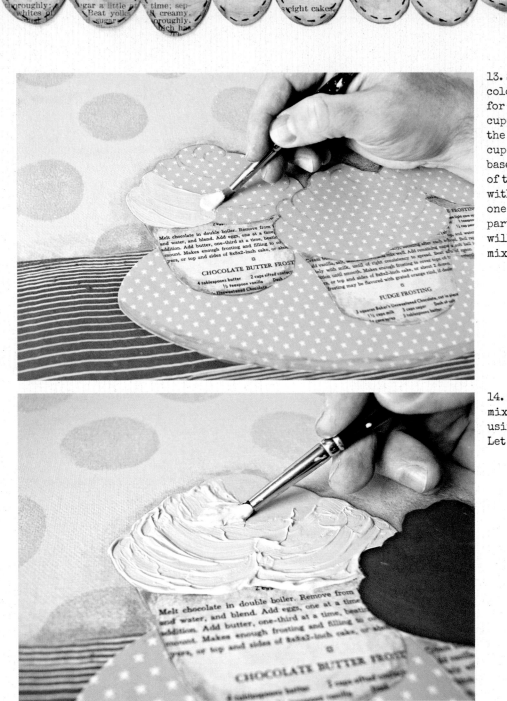

13. Select acrylic paint colors that you'd like for the frosting of the cupcakes. Then basecoat the frosting on each cupcake. While the basecoat dries, mix each of the frosting colors with molding paste using one part paint with two parts molding paste. This will be your frosting mixture.

14. Apply frosting mixture to each cupcake using a #8 round brush. Let dry overnight.

15. When the frosting is dry, adhere the flag picks with a dab of all-purpose glue.

16. Adhere the letters with all-purpose glue as well.

17. Use a hole punch and multitone papers to make confetti sprinkles. Apply the sprinkles randomly with dabs of all-purpose glue.

18. Adhere some pom-pom trim with all-purpose glue.

19. Drill holes in the top corners of the canvas for the hanging ribbon. Cut three equal lengths of seam binding or ribbon and feed the ends through the holes from back to front. We often use the back end of a very skinny paintbrush to push the ribbons through the holes. Then tie all three ribbon ends into a single knot to keep them from slipping back through the holes, making sure to leave some slack showing in front for a festive party-streamer effect.

This is certainly a piece you should be very proud of. And that's the reason we chose this fairly large format. It really does show off so many crafty talents all in one place. It's great for any room in the house, but we think it would be so fab in your little workspace, or even on the door to your studio or craft room.

SUPERCUTE MINI FAUX DOUGHNUTS

You can't help but feel a twinge of guilty pleasure when you start off a project by popping open a tub of Crayola clay. You're instantly transported back to childhood, messy hands and all. Faux sweets have a tendency to evoke smiles, and mini doughnuts are kinda at the top of the smile scale. As far as crafting goes, these embody the something-from-nothing method of creation. In the end you'll hardly believe that the perpetually perfect confections were once just globs of clay in your hands. And if you're looking for a project that the kiddos can help with, this is the one.

SUPPLIES

Crayola Air-Dry Clay

Heavy molding paste

Gloss varnish

#8 round brush

Craft mat or waxed paper

Cup of water

Acrylic paint

* pale yellow

* pink

* chocolate

* white

* tan

DIRECTIONS

1. This project requires some drying time between the sculpting step and the painting steps. So make sure to plan accordingly—these can't be last-minute gifts that you whip up the night before! To start, first lay down a craft sheet or a piece of waxed paper as a work surface. Then roll up equal-sized balls of clay, roughly the size of a golf ball.

2. Roll the ball into a log shape that's just long enough so that you can make the ends meet to make a mini doughnut.

3. Bend to make the ends meet.

4. Use your water to smooth your clay. A tiny dip of the finger works wonders. Smooth out the seam where you joined the two ends together.

5. Further smooth your doughnut with damp fingers.

6. Continue to shape and smooth the rest of your batch. Once you're done give them all a final once-over. Make them as smooth and round as possible. Let the clay fully dry for a couple of days. You'll know it's dry when the clay turns from gray to nearly pure white.

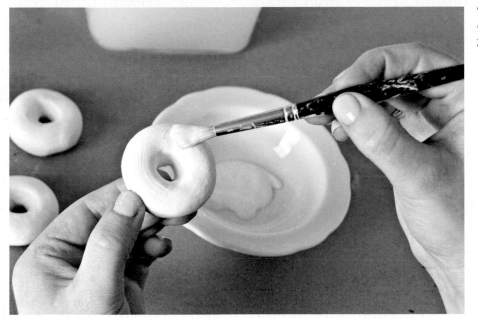

7. Basecoat the dry doughnuts with pale yellow and let dry.

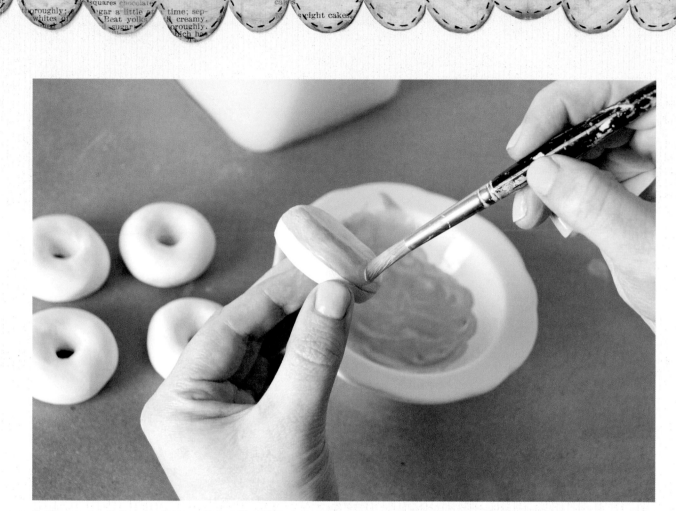

8. When actual doughnuts are fried they float on the surface of the oil and are flipped to brown each side. You'll notice a lighter tinted line that divides the doughnut. This is the part that wasn't fully submerged in oil. We call this the "fry line" and with some careful brushwork you can get this realistic look. First apply tan paint to half of your doughnut and then partially wipe it away with a paper towel to bring back some of the yellow. Ideally it'll look as if it's golden from the fryer.

9. When the first side is dry, do the same to the other side but leave a small strip of the pale yellow untouched. This is your "fry line," and it really adds to the realistic appearance.

10. Apply a clear coat of either decoupage medium or varnish to seal the doughnuts.

11. While the clear coat dries, mix up your glaze. We use one part paint, one part heavy gel medium and two parts gloss varnish. (So, half of the glaze is gloss varnish and the other half is evenly divided between paint and gel medium.) Use this as a starting point and adjust your glaze until it's a consistency that's dip-able without being too thick or too thin.

12. Dip your doughnut in about a third of the way.

13. Set your dipped doughnuts down flat to settle and dry. The peaks will go down and spread evenly for a realistic glazed look. Let the glaze dry overnight before handling. But before displaying or stacking, give them about a week to cure in order to prevent them from sticking together. These also make really cute magnets for the fridge. Hot-glue little magnets to the back to make some fabulously sweet home accessories.

You're going to pick up these little cuties about a million times once they're all dry and done. You can give them as gifts, all nestled in some tissue paper in a pink bakery box. Or display them on a tiny plate with a doily. What a cheery way to brighten your desk, countertop, vanity or windowsill.

YOUR VERY OWN MIXED MEDIA BRACELET

There's a distinct self-affirming pleasure in being your very own source material for future creative projects. The art you make today can be reproduced and repurposed in such a way to create the perfect give-and-take relationship with your work. Not to sound corny, but we like to think of the facets of this bracelet as the facets of your artistic development. A twist of the wrist is like turning a dial, or flipping back through the pages of your art journal. And you get to take all of that with you wherever you go. You'll look upon this piece of wearable art as a daily reminder of your unique creative talents.

SUPPLIES

Unfinished wooden bracelet
(We found great styles on etsy.com.)

Reduced photocopies of your
art journal pages (chapter 2)

Proportion wheel

Ruler

Decoupage medium

½"/1.3 cm flat brush

#2 round brush

#6 round brush

Gloss varnish

Mini rhinestones

Sanding pad

Acrylic paint
* white
* aqua
* pink
* burnt umber

DIRECTIONS

1. Measure the dimensions of your bracelet. Then select pages from your art journal and make reduced color copies to fit the dimensions of your bracelet. Because most copiers can only shrink an image to 25 percent, you may have to make second-generation copies like we did (meaning, make a reduced copy and then make a reduced copy of that copy). With the proportion wheel it's easy. (These are available on loan at most self-serve copy shops and can be bought there too.) Adjust the wheel to line up your beginning size with the size you'd like it to be. Or you can get all technologically fancy and do it the non-analog way with your home scanner and printer. But we went analog to show that it's doable for anyone.

2. Basecoat your bracelet. We first primed ours with white and then painted the inside aqua and the rim pink. Paint on all sides, inside and out, and let dry for 5–10 minutes.

3. Using decoupage medium adhere your cutout imagery to all sides of your bracelet and let dry for about 5 minutes.

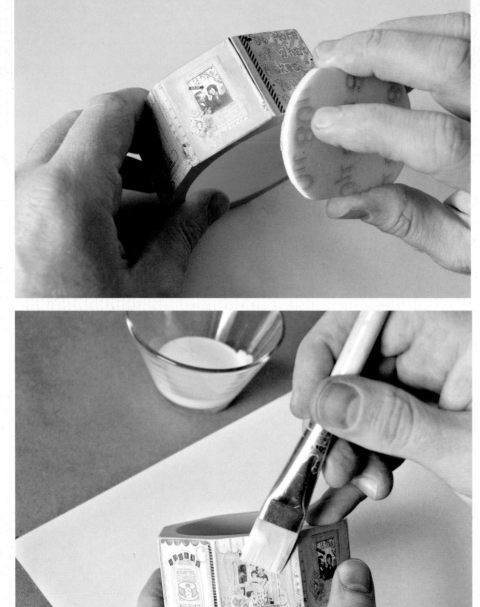

4. When dry use a sanding pad to sand off any excess paper edges and to smooth any rough paint. Dust off any particles.

5. Apply a topcoat of decoupage medium to the entire bracelet, inside and out. To avoid getting your hands too full, do only a portion at a time so there is always at least one dry spot to hold on to when you set the bracelet down to dry. Each portion should take about 5 minutes to dry.

6. Make an antique wash with one part burnt umber paint and two parts water, and then brush this over the surface of the bracelet. You can also make a white wash or a color wash using this same method. Go with the look you desire. Because you sealed it in the previous step, the wash will be easy to wipe off to the desired effect.

7. With a paper towel blot off the wash until you reach the desired effect.

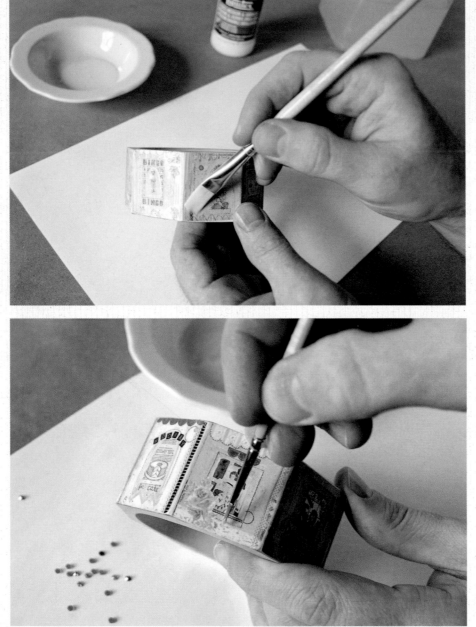

8. Apply a coat of gloss varnish to the entire surface of the bracelet. As before, do only a portion at a time so you are able to set it down. Let dry completely, approximately 10 minutes.

9. To adhere tiny rhinestones, use a #2 round brush to apply a small dot of the gloss varnish and then drop a rhinestone onto the dot of still-wet varnish.

10. Press down gently on each rhinestone and let dry. Our overall design is pretty subtle with the focus more on the texture and color of our teeny tiny art journal pages. But you can go all out with rhinestones and adornments if you like. Make your bracelet a representation of you and your art!

We hope this bridged the gaps for you between art journaling, crafting and jewelry making. There's a bit of each in this bracelet. It really is so cool to wear your own artwork . . . to look down and see your miniature handiwork captured under gloss upon your wrist.

HEIRLOOM BRIDE AND GROOM VINTAGE PHOTO ASSEMBLAGE

Two of our favorite collectibles are old photographs and vintage wedding cake toppers. So naturally this was the perfect starting point for an artful assemblage. And even though instant relatives (old photos found at flea markets and junk shops) generously inhabit our artwork and decor, we thought it would be all the more special to use actual relatives (Aaron's grandparents) in this little project that celebrates love and family. So dig through the family album, gather your supplies and create a piece of very personal and collectible art.

SUPPLIES

Oval wooden plaque

Wedding photo

Scissors

³⁄₄"/1.9 cm flat brush

#8 round brush

Hot glue gun

Distress Ink and applicator

Rickrack

Ruler

Millinery flowers

Watercolor paper

Sheet music

Patterned paper

Decoupage medium

All-purpose glue

Mini wood block

Wood veneer banner

Glass glitter

Clear glitter

Acrylic paint

* white

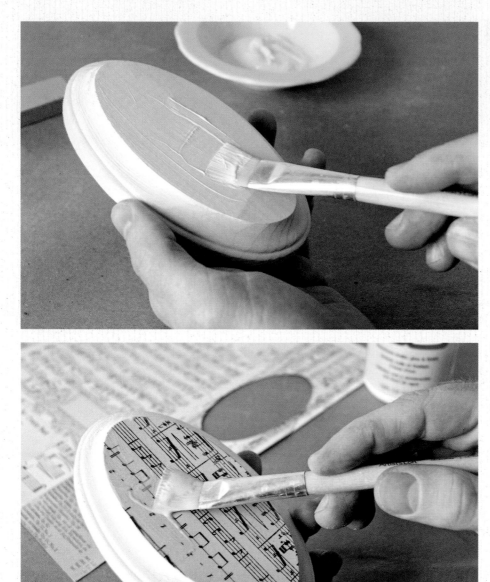

DIRECTIONS

1. Basecoat your plaque and mini wood block white and let dry for about 5 minutes. We selected a small oval because that's what best fit our photo.

2. With decoupage medium adhere sheet music or any patterned paper to your base. Let dry for about 5 minutes and then seal it with the medium.

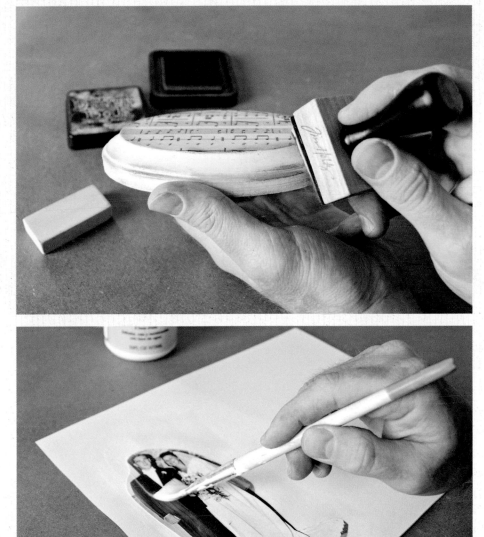

3. When dry to the touch, apply Distress Ink to the edges of your base and the mini block. We think everything is better with the patina of time—real or faux.

4. With decoupage medium adhere your happy couple to watercolor paper to bolster them. Let dry for about 5 minutes and then seal.

5. When dry to the touch, flip over your couple, adhere patterned paper to the back, let dry for 5 minutes and then seal. We try to always finish the backs of any project—even if it's going to be displayed where no one will ever see.

Then cut out your couple. Ours has some dress pooling on the floor, which is the portion we glued to the base. If yours does not have a pooling dress, then try to cut out a portion of the floor in front of the couple.

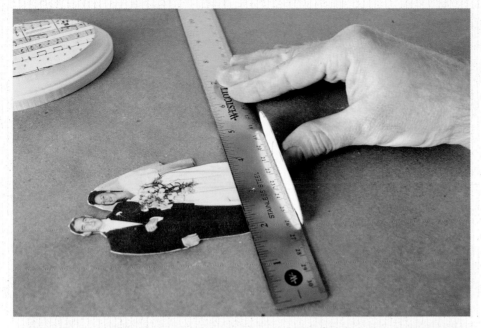

6. We folded the pooled dress portion of the dress forward using a ruler to get a crisp fold. Again, any portion of the photograph's foreground will suffice.

7. Adhere some millinery flowers or other accessories with hot glue.

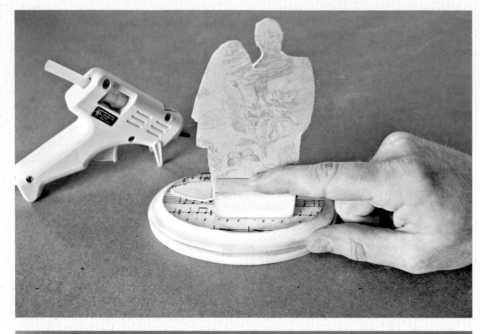

8. Use a hot glue gun to attach the couple to the base. Then hot-glue the mini block right behind the couple for support.

9. Use all-purpose glue to attach your rickrack trim to the base. Because ours is a mostly black-and-white theme, we thought silver worked well.

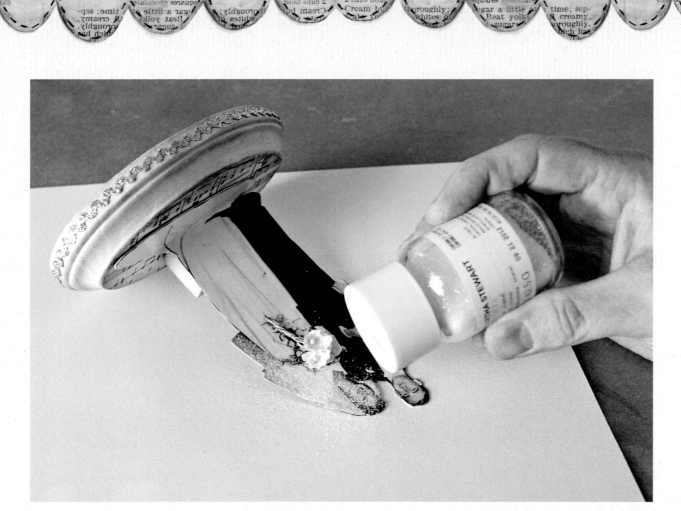

10. Brush a light coat of decoupage medium onto the veil and then sprinkle with clear glitter. Use glitter to adorn a top hat, a portion of a dress, etc. This detail makes all the difference.

11. Adhere some glass glitter around the base of your couple for even more shimmery magic.

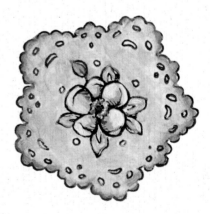

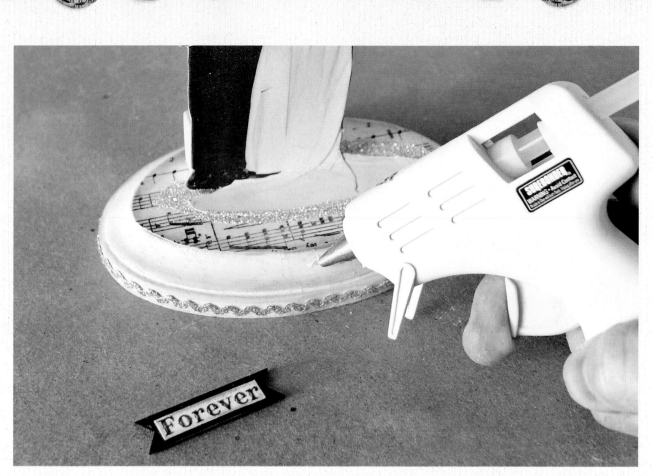

12. Finish off your piece with a fabulous decorative banner. Attach it to the base with hot glue.

This piece makes a perfect anniversary gift or valentine, or you can even create your own custom wedding cake topper. Little shelf sitters like this are the key elements in many collections. What a great way to give some real attention to that photograph that was maybe hidden in a shoe box for years.

SWEET SPOT NECKLACE

Every art journal page has a sweet spot. That little area where all the right colors, patterns, textures and elements come together to define the overall aesthetic of the page. Finding this sweet spot can be a rewarding creative venture in itself. As we flipped through our pages, clear necklace charm in hand, gliding it over the colorful surfaces like crafty cartographers, we found new appreciation for our art journaling process.

In this project you'll closely examine the artful minutiae of your methods and make that the focal point of this fabulous piece of handmade jewelry.

SUPPLIES

Clear plastic charms

Pink mini-ball chain

Jump ring

Bail

Wooden beads

Felt heart bead

Photocopy of a journal page or pages (chapter 2)

Paper ephemera

Patterned paper

Sanding pad

E6000 adhesive

#6 round brush

¾"/1.9 cm flat brush

Pencil

Scissors

Decoupage medium

Acrylic paint

* black

* pink

* cream

* metallic gold

DIRECTIONS

1. Select your clear plastic charms, and find the sweet spots in your journal that you'd like to immortalize.

2. Instead of cutting up your beloved art journal, make color copies of your selected pages and then use your charm as a template to trace the shape onto the copy.

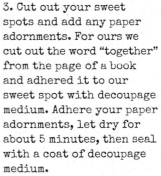

3. Cut out your sweet spots and add any paper adornments. For ours we cut out the word "together" from the page of a book and adhered it to our sweet spot with decoupage medium. Adhere your paper adornments, let dry for about 5 minutes, then seal with a coat of decoupage medium.

4. When the sealer coat is dry to the touch, about 5 minutes, add some details with paint. Add little bits of pink on the cheeks, or add color to otherwise black-and-white clothing. Use your detail brush and tiny bits of paint to add whatever flourishes you desire. Let dry for about 5 minutes.

5. Apply an even coat of decoupage medium to the face of your sweet spot and press to adhere it to the surface of the charm so that the image is sealed to the charm and the plain paper back is exposed. You can apply pressure with a dry paper towel to aid in smoothing out any air bubbles that may be between the image and the charm. Don't panic if it looks white and cloudy, because the medium will dry clear.

6. To dress up the back, adhere patterned paper with decoupage medium. Let dry for about 5 minutes and use a sanding pad to sand off any excess paper edges. Then seal the back with decoupage medium.

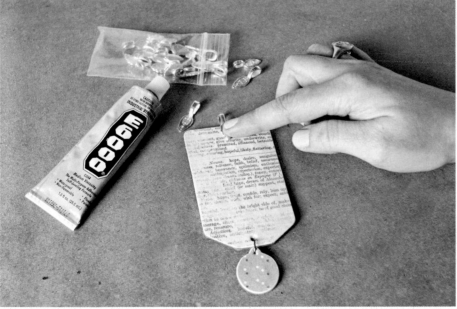

7. Because we have two charms, we connected them with a jump ring and then glued a bail to the back. To attach your bail, apply a dab of E6000, press down the bail and let dry fully, about 10 minutes.

8. Now you'll paint the wooden beads, let them dry and then speckle them with paint. A good way to handle the beads when painting and speckling is to put the beads on the handle end of a skinny paintbrush. To speckle, mix one part paint with two parts water, dip your #6 round brush into this wash and then hold the brush a few inches away from the bead. Tap the metal part of the brush so that paint speckles the bead.

9. When the painted and speckled beads are dry to the touch, apply a topcoat of decoupage medium. Let dry for about 5 minutes.

10. String your charms and beads onto your chain. We think ours is fairly basic and yet still a stand-out piece. You can go as subtle or elaborate as you like.

There you have it: Ten steps and now you've got a piece of jewelry—made by you! Whether this is your entry into jewelry making or just a change from your previous methods, this necklace is that much more special because it captures a piece of your very own art journal.

FAUXBULOUS KEEPSAKE CAKE

We consider this faux cake to be the ultimate BIG craft project. When you see it completed, in all of its magical glory, you're apt to wonder, "Where would I even begin?"

And we'll admit that it was once intimidating to us. But seriously, you can toss any fear aside. This is a project that utilizes entry-level skills to produce expert-level results. And the stress-free fun you'll have along the way will make the finished prize even sweeter.

The themes you can go with are endless, as are the colors—or shall we say *flavors*? In a perfect world we'd have faux cakes on every available surface. On cake stands, under cloches, topped with twirling ballerinas and swirls of everlasting frosting. Well, here's to making the world more perfect!

SUPPLIES

Three 8"/20.3 cm Styrofoam disks

10"/25.4 cm wooden circle for cake base

Painter's acrylic latex caulk

Kitchen utility knife

Small spatula

Palette knife

Ruler

Pencil

Scissors

Tracing paper

Watercolor paper

Piping image template (Page 169)

Patterned paper

#8 round brush

Sharpie pen

X-Acto knife

Stripy paper straws

Rickrack

Stage curtain collage sheet

Ballerina cupcake toppers

Wood veneer stars and spots

Crystal-clear glitter

Pom-pom trim

All-purpose glue

Decoupage medium

Distress Ink and applicator

Plastic rose cupcake picks

Acrylic paint

* pink

* pale yellow

* light brown

DIRECTIONS

1. Stack your three Styrofoam disks, find the center and mark with a pencil. This will be your guide for cutting the cake.

2. Use a kitchen utility knife to cut out a quarter of the cake.

3. Scoop an entire tube of caulk into a bowl. This will be your frosting. Add acrylic paint to tint it to your liking, and use a palette knife or small spatula to stir it up. A little paint goes a long way, so add just a few drops at a time. If you want to do chocolate, first check out the already-tinted varieties at the home improvement store. They have browns that look just like chocolate frosting.

4. Apply the frosting between the layers of your cake and stack as you go.

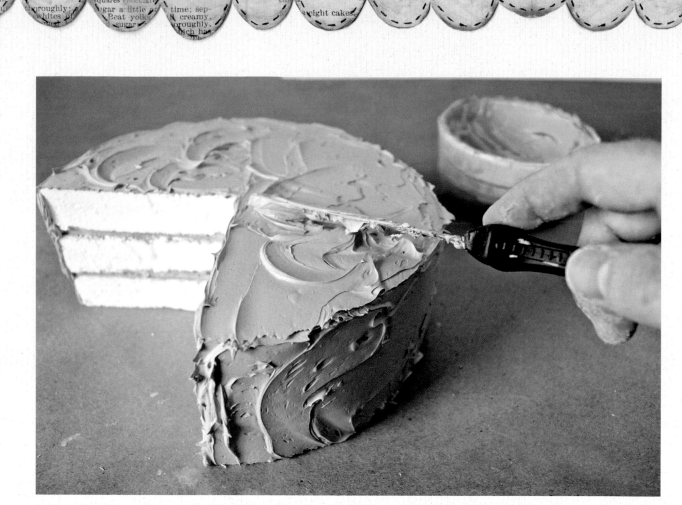

5. Then frost the entire exterior of the cake the same way you would a real cake. Once you've got it looking how you want, set it aside and let it dry overnight.

6. When your frosting is completely dry it will be rubbery but not movable. Use a #8 round brush to paint the interior of your cake and let dry for about 5 minutes. You may need two coats because Styrofoam is a fairly thirsty surface.

7. Make a light brown wash using one part paint with two parts water. Use your #8 round brush to apply the wash a small section at a time around the edges of the cake layers to give your layers a golden, baked appearance. This is the process for golden cake, but if you decide to do chocolate layers, then simply paint them brown.

8. With a clean but damp #8 round brush, blend the light brown wash to soften the appearance.

9. Let dry for about 5 minutes and then apply a sealing coat of decoupage medium.

10. Set your cake aside for now. Then cut out patterned paper and adhere to the top of your base with decoupage medium. Let dry for about 5 minutes and then seal.

11. Antique the edges of the base with Distress Ink. (We just love Distress Ink!) Tap the applicator to the ink pad and then scuff the edges of your surface with the applicator.

Fauxbulous Keepsake Cake 69

12. Attach some fun rickrack to the rim of the base with all-purpose glue.

13. Now that your base is done, let's get back to the cake. First trace the piping template onto tracing paper, and then flip your tracing paper to heavily trace the lines on the other side so you can then transfer the lines onto patterned paper.

14. With a smooth, blunt object, such as the back end of a Sharpie marker, rub your tracing onto patterned paper.

15. Trace over your piping lines with a Sharpie pen and cut out.

16. Use all-purpose glue to adhere your piping to the bottom rim of the cake.

17. To bolster your paper curtains, first adhere them to watercolor paper with decoupage medium. Then doodle some accents with a Sharpie pen, and draw some guidelines for when you will later cut out the curtains. Add a ¼"/6.4 mm tab to the outside edge—this will slip into the straws that hold up the curtains. Before you cut out your curtains, adhere some patterned paper to the flipside of them. We like when our projects look finished from 360 degrees.

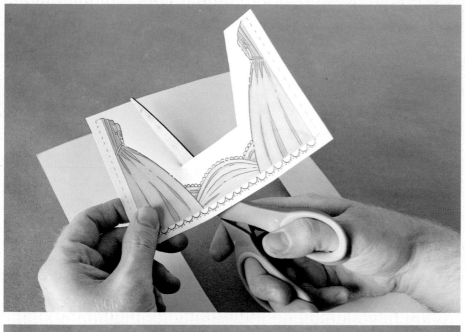

18. Cut out your curtains, making sure to leave the ¼"/6.4 mm tab on the edges that will slide into the straws.

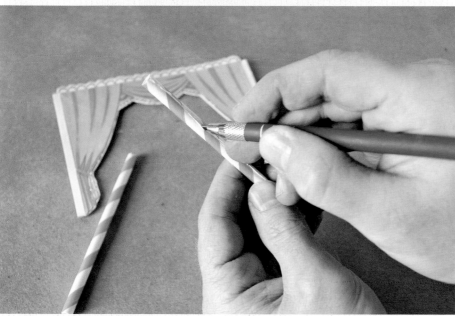

19. Cut your straws to the proper height, about ½"/1.3 cm taller than your curtains, so that there will be extra length at the bottom that will stick into the cake and hold the curtains in place. Use an X-Acto knife to slice directly down the center lengthwise, making sure that you don't cut all the way through to the other side of the straw.

20. Slide your ¼"/6.4 mm tab into the slots you cut in your straws, making sure to leave the extra ½"/1.3 cm on the bottom.

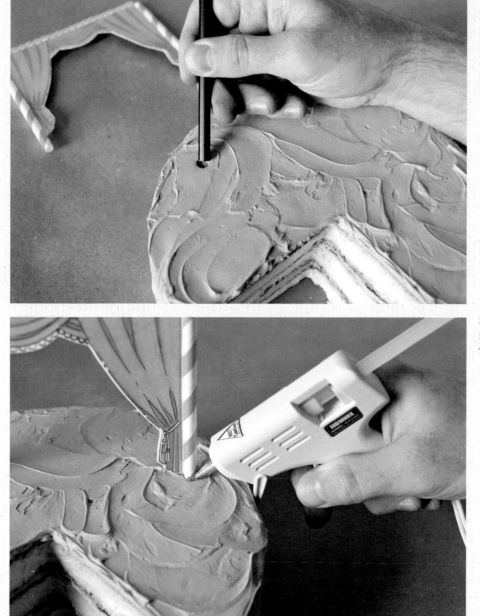

21. Position your curtains atop your cake and make little dots with a pencil as guides. Then poke holes into your cake in the marked spots using a dull pencil.

22. Insert the straw ends into the holes and secure with a bit of hot glue.

Fauxbulous Keepsake Cake   75

23. Now poke your roses into the cake. We wanted ours flanking the curtains.

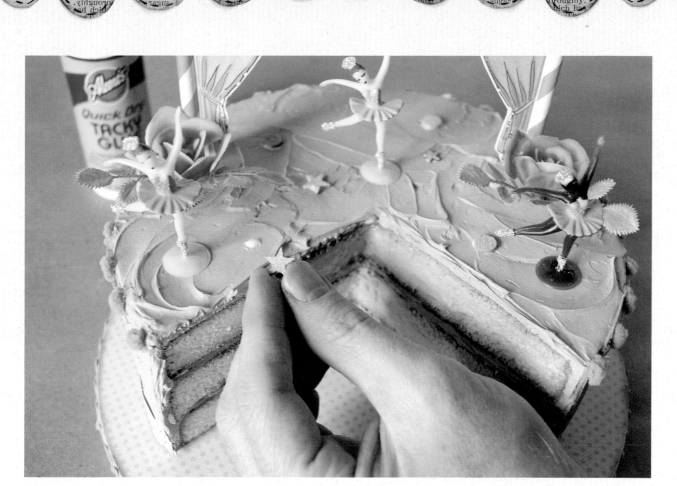

24. Use all-purpose glue to attach your ballerinas. And really, the details are up to you. We glittered some colorful little wood veneer stars and dots and placed them around like sprinkles.

Faux cakes are fixtures in our home, and one like this evokes a festive mood whenever you see it. What a great project to do for a kid's birthday party—a cake he or she can keep forever to remember the special day! You should be proud of your crafty self for making such a fab project, and we know that you won't stop at one cake. Before long you'll have one in every flavor and variety!

CHAPTER 2

For the LOVE of Art Journaling

For more years than these two youngsters would like to admit, we've been working artists. Since getting our first apartment only months out of high school, our sole means of supporting ourselves relied on what we could do with paint, paintbrushes and the like. But this isn't about the struggles of the *starving artist*. The questions we're posing are: When you make art to live, can you still *live* to make art? Can the thing you *have* to do, be the thing you *love* to do?

For us, there is one answer to these questions, and it lies between the pages of our art journals. These bloated books are filled with paint, paper, ink, charcoal, photos, glue, glitter, washi tape and everything else. Their spines crack from overuse and artistic abuse. These creatively saturated pages have nothing to do with a career in art and everything to do with an artful escape.

Art is personal, as is a journal. So it follows that an art journal is about as personal as you can get. We would never claim to be able to teach someone to *be* an artist. But we certainly can impart a great deal of wisdom, tips, tricks, hints and inspiration that we've culled from more than eighteen years (there . . . we said it!) as working artists who still *live* to make art. As you'll come to see in the following pages, your art journal is where you can do anything you want. Maybe you can't go out and shop for all the things you want . . . the clothes, the decor, the art. Maybe you can't dye your hair pink, wear bold makeup or travel the world. But in a way you can do these things in your art journal. With your own hands you can artfully render your wishes, dreams, memories, obsessions and greatest passions. And they can be as clean, messy, beautiful, strange, outrageous or lovely as you'd like them to be.

LOVELY LADY LAYERS AND LINES

We love the art of combining seemingly disparate elements to create something that's not only aesthetically cohesive, but also much more appealing than the sum of its parts. In other words, this project is all you, and we aim to free you of any fears you might have about drawing or detail painting.

It begins with a collage of pretty paper that's merely the backdrop to your bold-lined, hand-painted portrait, rendered with nods to Banksy, Shepard Fairey, Lichtenstein and vintage sewing patterns. And the best part is that you don't need to be an expert with a pencil or paintbrush. We provide the lovely lady to get you started—you just have to fill in the lines. This one is sure to build your rendering confidence, especially in wielding a detail brush. In the end you'll have a journal page worthy of framing.

SUPPLIES

Patterned paper

Tracing paper

#5 round brush

#8 round brush

3/4"/1.9 cm flat brush

Charcoal pencil (medium or soft)

Pencil

Scissors

Decoupage medium

Gesso

Acrylic paint

* gloss black
* pale gray
* pale pink
* berry pink
* burnt umber
* white

Lovely Lady image template (see page 170)

DIRECTIONS

1. Select an assortment of monochromatic patterned paper, preferably with subtle patterns and colors. Tear them and arrange them on your page, positioning the least bold pattern where the face will be in the center of the page. We like the way our pale polka dots channel a Lichtenstein girl.

2. Adhere the paper to your page with decoupage medium and smooth out any wrinkles and bubbles. Let your collage dry for about 5 minutes, then apply a topcoat of decoupage medium, making sure to fully cover your collage so that it is protected from washes that you'll be applying.

3. Make a white wash using one part acrylic paint or gesso with two parts water. Brush the wash over your collage and blot with a paper towel until the collage has a muted effect.

4. You may need to resize your Lovely Lady image template (see page 170) on a copier so that it fits your journal page. Then place tracing paper over the image and outline the lines in pencil. Turn your tracing paper over and retrace the lines on the reverse side of the tracing paper, pressing hard so that the pencil lines will transfer clearly in the next step. Do this on top of some scrap paper so that the pencil doesn't transfer to your tabletop.

5. Flip the tracing paper so that the image is facing the same way as the original and position the tracing on your collaged page using some tape to keep it from shifting. Rub your tracing onto the page using a smooth, blunt object. We like to use the back end of a Sharpie marker. Rub hard and thoroughly because the better your transfer is, the easier it will be to paint.

6. While rubbing on your lines, carefully pull back a corner of the tracing paper, without shifting it, so that you can check to see how well the image is transferring.

7. Keep your image template close by for visual reference when painting. Start by painting in the gray areas using your #5 round brush.

8. When the gray is dry to the touch, about 5 minutes, paint in the glossy black areas with the same brush, and then finish up by painting in the lipstick color.

9. Make an antique wash using one part burnt umber with two parts water. Apply to the edges and corners of your page with a brush and blot with a paper towel until you achieve the desired effect.

10. Speckling, or paint flecking, is one of our go-to art journaling effects, and in this project it gives the look of overspray or sputtering from a spray can. To speckle, dip your #8 round brush into the antique wash, then hold your loaded brush a few inches in the air above your page. Tap the metal part of your brush so that the wash spits onto your page. Avoid speckling the face, but if you do so accidentally you can wipe it away with a paper towel because your page has been sealed.

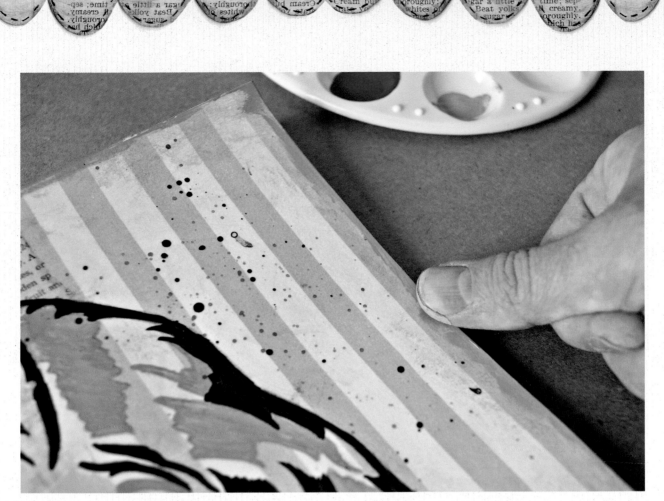

11. To distress with paint, use your thumb or finger to rub the edges of your page with a corresponding paint color. In our case, the pink looks best with our pink-themed collage. Let the paint dry completely.

12. With a soft or medium charcoal pencil, trace around the silhouette of your lady, rubbing with the side of the sharpened tip.

13. Fade the charcoal outward with your finger or paper towel to give it a hazy effect. This step enhances the stenciled graffiti look of your image and also pulls the portrait forward a bit from the background.

Of all the classes we've taught around the United States, this one elicited the most satisfaction from our students. After all, the hardest part about painting faces is daring to try. These simple methods of line tracing and painting with solid colors can be applied to many portrait-style projects. Collage and paint a canvas to hang in your home—or frame the fabulous page you just created! For future portraits, you can look online to find an endless supply of pretty faces in the graphics of vintage sewing patterns.

FAVORITE THINGS

Your Favorite Things page should be an absolute labor of love. Well, your whole art journal should be . . . but this page is the one that is sure to bring you the most pleasure. We had a lot of fun with it and it was so easy to find inspiration—it was all around us! Our striped walls just had to be the background, and our huge collection of vintage stuffed bunnies would definitely make an appearance. We for sure had to include a Charlotte doll, and looking around our home at all of the bottlebrush trees and cupcakes made those two a shoe-in. Maybe the only hard part was leaving things off the page. But don't think you have to leave anything out. Dedicate this page to the things that make you smile all the time.

SUPPLIES

Texture Crackle medium

Assorted ephemera

Images of some of your favorite things

Dimensional sticker letters

#8 round brush

¾"/1.9 cm flat brush

Palette knife or old gift card

Sharpie pen

Assorted stamps

Black ink pad

Rickrack

Patterned paper

Watercolor paper

Colored thread

Sewing needle

Decorative letters

Decoupage medium

Distress Ink and applicator

All-purpose glue

Acrylic paint

* pink
* white
* tan
* aqua
* burnt umber
* black

DIRECTIONS

1. Basecoat your page with tan paint, and when that is dry, about 5-10 minutes, seal it with a clear coat. This step is necessary as an undercoat for the white Texture Crackle. When it crackles you'll see the contrasting tan in the cracks, and you can use any color you like. When the clear coat is dry to the touch, about 5 minutes, apply a thin coat of the Texture Crackle, just enough so that it's opaque. Use a palette knife to apply it, or use an old gift card like we did.

2. When the Texture Crackle dries you will have a gorgeously crackled page surface to work upon. We decided to paint stripes for our background. To do this, use a ruler to measure, and lightly draw the pencil lines 1½"/3.8 cm apart. But you can also freehand it if that's your style.

3. Paint in your stripes. Because the theme of this page is Favorite Things, we just had to go with pink and white stripes as a backdrop. We have had pink-and-white striped walls in every home we ever lived in together!

4. After the stripes are dry to the touch, about 5-10 minutes, apply a clear coat to the page to seal it. Then apply an antique wash using two parts water with one part tan or brown paint. Apply the wash with a paint-brush, concentrating on corners and edges a bit more than the center of the page.

5. You can use a paper towel to blot the wash off to the desired effect. We love how the wash settles in the cracks.

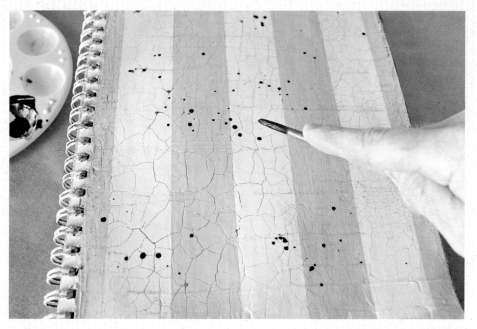

6. We love the way black speckles look against the sweet pink and white stripes. To speckle, mix one part paint with two parts water, dip a paintbrush into the mix, then hold the brush that's loaded with the wash over the page and tap the metal part of the brush with your finger so that the wash speckles the page.

7. Draw your caption with pencil on watercolor paper. It doesn't matter how wonky your caption is—just freehand it and love it.

8. Paint your caption in a color that you think works well with your background.

9. Speckle your caption, and use Distress Ink to burnish the edges. Distress Ink gives elements an aged look, and it will make them stand out even more against your backdrop.

10. Stitch around your caption with some thread. We really wanted our caption to be special, and we thought a sewed-on look works perfectly.

11. Set your caption aside, and let's get back to the page. Scallop borders along the top of the page work well, especially combined with the stripes. Apply the scallop with some decoupage medium and then seal it.

12. And now it's time for the stars of the show: a few of your favorite things gathered at the bottom of the page. Group your favorite things however you like. Apply a clear coat to protect the images.

13. We love distressing the page with paint, and it takes nothing more than dipping a fingertip in color and smearing it where you think a bit of pink, aqua, white or whatever is needed. Also brush a bit of an antique wash around your elements and below the scallop to make them come forward from the background a bit.

14. For us it wouldn't be a Favorite Things page without some black stamps as accents and of course some doodles and a few words done in Sharpie pen. Use arrow stamps to point to your favorite things and add notes about your collections and why you love them.

15. Ahh, we love flocking powder. It has such a soft, plushy look and all it takes to apply is a bit of decoupage medium. Brush the medium onto the desired areas, then shake out some of the powder and tap off the excess. It's so cool to go back later and feel the soft fuzzy parts of your page. Imagine making your very own touch-and-feel children's book!

16. It's time to add the pomp and circumstance to your Favorite Things spread! Add some bold title lettering with all-purpose glue . . . or even use some dimensional sticker letters like we did on our caption. Glue on some metallic accents, maybe some rickrack along the bottom of the page, and with dabs of decoupage medium you can apply tiny gold stars here and there for shimmery highlights. Don't you love how the stitches around the caption make it look as if it's sewn to the page?

Your inspirations often change. So art journaling those things that are your favorites is not only fun but maybe even necessary for keeping track of your creative development. Your favorite things of today may not be your favorite things a few years from now. You're constantly evolving, but it's useful to look back and draw from your past influences. On another note, using Texture Crackle is nearly addictive! It's such a great mood setting surface to work upon.

I SEE A WHITE PAGE AND I WANT TO PAINT IT BLACK

In our art journal we mainly use black as an accent . . . in bits of lettering, doodles, outlines and stamps. But there's something very interesting about starting with a black page and working from there. So to switch things up a bit, you'll begin by painting your entire page black. We think you'll be surprised when you lay down your go-to elements and see that they are so much more striking. Pull out your favorite paint colors and against the black you see them in a whole new light. In a way, everything looks even better, but at the same time it's a bit daunting. The challenge here is in trying to get all of your elements and colors to work well together. It's really such a simple concept, but we think you'll find a new love for working on top of black. It's time to step outside your comfort zone and make some stunning art in the process.

SUPPLIES

Scissors

Vintage photograph

Paper photo corners

Paper ephemera

Assorted patterned paper

Doily stamp

Two pastel ink pads

Two patterned stamps

Bottle caps

Wood veneer talk bubble and mini shapes

Washi tape

Black-and-white baker's twine

¾"/1.9 cm flat brush

#8 round brush

Sharpie pen

Decoupage medium

All-purpose glue

Glass glitter

Acrylic paint

* black

* aqua

* cream

* pink

DIRECTIONS

1. Well, what did you think the first step would be? With your ³/₄"/1.9 cm brush paint your page black and let dry.

2. Figure out where you'd like the focal point of your page to be. This is where your "pileup" will appear. With two or three paint colors of your choice, apply paint to your stamps with a brush and stamp a random overlapping pattern.

3. Adhere your patterned paper accents using decoupage medium. The bit of book text that we used is one of our go-to patterns because it's neutral and has great texture. Also, random scallops cut from patterned paper and applied to the top and bottom borders will carry your theme to the edges of your page.

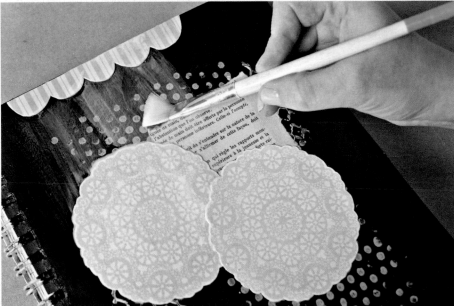

4. To start a pileup like this, stamp two pastel doily patterns onto watercolor paper and cut them out. Then adhere them with decoupage medium, making sure to leave some of your previous paint stamping peeking out. When dry, apply a topcoat of decoupage medium to the entire page and let dry.

5. Add texture by brushing some paint onto the rim of a bottle cap and stamping the page. The less perfect the better.

6. With your #8 round brush speckle the page with bright-colored paints. First thin your paint using two parts water with one part paint. Dip your brush into this wash, hold the brush a few inches in the air above your page and tap the metal part of your brush so that the paint speckles the page.

7. Preserve your vintage photos by first making photocopies of them. Then adhere the photocopy to watercolor paper to bolster it. You can add decorative photo corners for extra pop, and then apply to your page pileup using all-purpose glue. Add a strip of washi tape to your photo to give it a taped-in look, and add a strip along the binding.

8. With all-purpose glue apply your paper ephemera and accent the page with 3-D elements such as the baker's twine.

9. Adorn your mini wood veneer shapes with glass glitter by applying a dab of all-purpose glue, sprinkling with glass glitter and shaking off the excess. When dry, apply these glittery accents to your page with all-purpose glue.

10. Paint a wood veneer talk bubble and add words using cutout letters or stamps. Then adhere to your page with all-purpose glue.

11. Distress the edges of your page with paint. Dip the tip of your finger in paint and then rub along the rim of the page, bringing color and texture to the edge of your page.

12. For a final bit of texture add stitching to your scallop borders using a Sharpie pen.

We hope you get hooked on using black for a little while. It makes for such a bold look in your art journaling. You can even go with a matte black surface and use chalk for a blackboard theme. If you had fun doing this, then you should take a few minutes to flip through your art journal and paint some random pages black throughout. That way, any day you feel like starting out with a black page the initial step is done already.

I WONDER WHAT SHE WISHED FOR

The childhood birthday photograph. Would there even be photo albums or scrapbooks if not for these? We capture these special moments between the covers of a book because they are so very fleeting and essential at the same time. Photographs tie the generations together in ways that words cannot express, and childhood birthday photos are always so magical, especially those from the previous generation. We thought that this would be a fabulous starting point for an art journal page . . . to gather the images and dreams of family and childhood together, and artfully give them a new and colorful meaning.

SUPPLIES

Birthday photos

Patterned paper

Watercolor paper

Scissors

#8 round brush

#6 round brush

¾"/1.9 cm flat brush

Assorted stamps

Bubble Wrap

Wood block stamp

Black ink pad

Decoupage medium

All-purpose glue

Dimensional lettering

Chipboard accents

Black-and-white baker's twine

Imagery and assorted ephemera

Sharpie pen

Acrylic paint

* pink

* aqua

* brown

* white

* tan

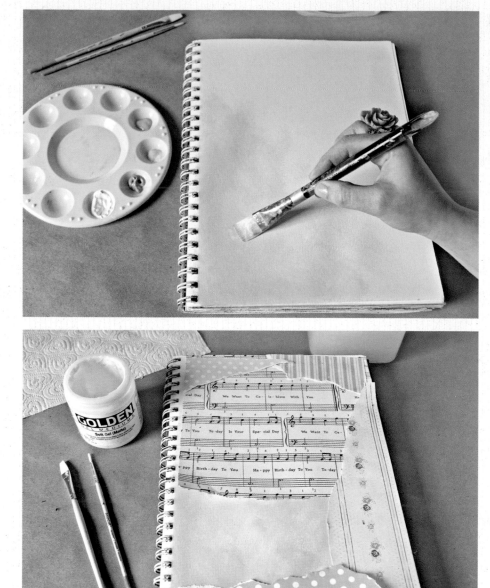

DIRECTIONS

1. The background of this page is a combination of paper collage and paint. This time we wanted to start with the paint. Select colors that work well with your paper and blend them on your page with your ¾"/1.9 cm flat brush. There really are no rules—just blend one color into the next, going for a soft, wash-like appearance.

2. Tear your paper pieces and lay them out on the page with a rough idea of your overall layout.

3. Use decoupage medium to adhere your paper collage and your photos. Let dry for about 5 minutes, then add a topcoat of the medium to seal the entire collaged page.

4. Vintage photos have white borders that work perfectly to frame them upon a colorful page. But as you can see here, our photos are placed on top of an area that's mostly white. To make these photos pop, paint the white borders with bright-colored paint. On ours, this also works as a tie-in to the color at the bottom of the page. And don't worry about being neat with your paintbrush. Going outside the lines adds more character.

5. To age and mute the page, apply watered-down light tan paint and then blend with a fingertip over pretty much the entire page except for the photos. This step will make your focal images stand out more in the end.

6. To age the page a bit more, add watered-down darker tan paint to the edges of the page in the same way as the previous step. You can use a paper towel to blot and wipe away the applied paint until you get the desired antique-y look.

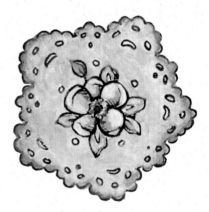

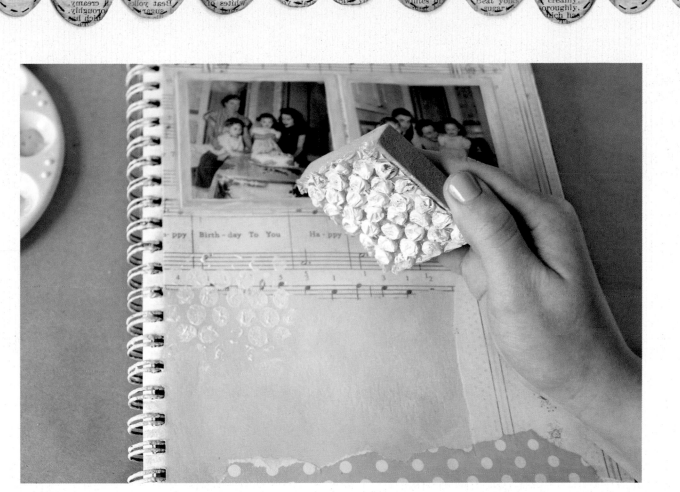

7. Bubble wrap is great for adding texture with paint. Our homemade stamp consists of bubble wrap glued to a wood block. Apply some white paint and stamp it on your page in a haphazard manner.

8. Speckling never ever gets old for us. And using sepia-toned speckles is an easy way to add an aged and distressed look. To speckle, create a wash with two parts water and one part paint. Dip a small or medium round brush in this wash, hold the loaded brush above the page and tap the metal part of the brush so that the wash sprays upon the page.

9. We absolutely love these faux cup ring stamps for "messing up" the page a bit more.

10. Add your decorative elements, a piece at a time, figuring out the best placement for your theme. Add color with a detail brush if needed. We wanted the cake plate a bit more aqua.

11. With all-purpose glue add some chipboard elements like this adorable balloon to give the page more dimension. Attach a bit of dangling string for a whimsical feel.

12. All along you want to keep in mind where your lettering might end up. We made color copies of vintage board game letters and adhered them with all-purpose glue. You can use Scrabble pieces, your favorite chipboard letters, whatever works on your page.

13. And a page isn't complete without some doodles. Sketching faux stitching around photos is one of our go-to methods for adding texture and interest. Little bits of black are striking against a pastel background.

You'll soon see that memories are a big part of the art journaling process. With a page like this you get to re-create that lost childhood magic. It's not really something you can express with words . . . those glimmering dreamy birthday party moments. And when there aren't words, there is art.

I taught myself to bake

*when in doubt, make extra frosting!

*know your measurements

*always level off your cups

*Real ingredients are best.

Extreme Chocolate Cake

· buttercream frosting

· decorative piping

· classic golden cake

I TAUGHT MYSELF TO BAKE

Baking is a recurring theme in our work, and it's not just for the delicious aesthetics. There's something about the act of baking itself that has been a saving grace in our home. It's afforded us that little bit of escape needed from the workday while still allowing us to stay creative. And there's no place that the art of baking is celebrated more than in vintage recipe books. Their pages are a study in patience, tried-and-true practices and tradition. With so little available media in the '30s and '40s, these books were possibly the sole source of this specialized information for homemakers of that time. We wanted this page to be a celebration of bliss in the kitchen and the time-honored act of baking the right way. And before you embark, please try to take the time to hunt down some fab vintage wallpaper for this spread (Etsy.com is a great place to start). For a warm, homey collage there's nothing better than tattered and time-faded wallpaper bits.

SUPPLIES

Vintage wallpaper

Patterned paper

Watercolor paper

Title lettering

Dimensional stickers

Decorative lace trim frame

Vintage baking gal photo

Cake images

Sharpie pen

Scissors

#8 round brush

#4 round brush

¾"/1.9 cm flat brush

Gesso

Decoupage medium

All-purpose glue

Acrylic paint

* aqua

* tan

* pink

* white

* burnt umber

* gray

DIRECTIONS

1. Brush some patches of paint on your page in colors that will work well with the collage you're going to create next. Even though most of the page will be covered with paper, some painted areas will peek through and give the page a layered look.

2. To collage a page like this we love the look of torn paper. And in this case we happened to have some gorgeous vintage wallpaper pieces to use. Because it's a baking theme we thought these vintage wallpaper designs that would've adorned the walls of an old-fashioned kitchen worked well. Adhere whatever paper you choose with decoupage medium and let dry for about 5 minutes. Then seal with a topcoat.

3. Apply gesso to mute the paper collage a bit and give it texture. Brush it on in a varied, haphazard manner.

4. Because you sealed your collage earlier, you'll be able to blot off any of the gesso with a paper towel to give it a softer look.

5. Adhere and seal a piece of patterned paper with recipe book clippings in the center of the page. This will be where you place your focal image. A great way to add importance to your focal point is to cut these paper pieces with clean lines that will stand out against the torn collage background.

6. Prepare the header on your page. We made ours by sketching out a simple rolling pin shape and then tracing the lines onto some tracing paper.

7. Trace the lines onto pattern paper so that your header design brings more color and texture to the page.

8. Adhere your patterned paper design to water-color paper to bolster it. To add some dimension, use a #4 round brush to float in a shadow using a basic paint wash of one part paint with two parts water in either a gray or dark brown. Brush a light wash along the bottom of the image to mimic a shadow.

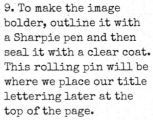

9. To make the image bolder, outline it with a Sharpie pen and then seal it with a clear coat. This rolling pin will be where we place our title lettering later at the top of the page.

10. Now back to the page. To speckle the page, make a wash with two parts water and one part paint, dip in a #8 round brush and then hold the loaded brush above the page and tap the metal part of the brush so that the wash speckles the page. Let the paint dry for 5–10 minutes. Adhere your images using decoupage medium and then apply sealer.

11. Add some great color and texture with a bit of smeared paint. Dip your fingertip in color and then rub along the edges of the page. Let the smeared paint dry for about 5 minutes, until it's dry to the touch. Then add any decorative elements, such as the rolling pin header. We added lettering to ours. And dimensional stickers always make a page fun.

12. A page like this wouldn't be complete without some doodled lettering. The little bits of handy baking notes tie the page together.

13. Use a charcoal pencil to render some drop shadows beneath your decorative elements. Sketch and then blend smooth with your fingertip. This will make the images pop out a bit against the background.

14. After looking over the page you may find that something is missing. In this case we thought a scallop border along the top would look perfect. Use your #3 round brush to paint it on. Freehand it—it doesn't matter how imperfect it is. Once dry to the touch, about 5–10 minutes, use your Sharpie to doodle an outline. Finally, use your charcoal pencil as you did previously to add a drop shadow. Again, sketch and blend with your fingertip.

Baking is such a great theme for an art journal. We have found so many old homemade recipe books over the years that nearly resemble art journals . . . there are recipes on index cards glued in, pictures from cake mix boxes or magazines, little sketches of frosting techniques. There's just something so homey and blissfully domestic in the baking arts. And making art from baking brings that feeling full circle.

DOWN THE SHORE

Ahh, sweet escapes! Whether big or small, short or long, they've got the power to restore our souls to their upright positions. We're lucky here on the Jersey Shore, being mere minutes from our beloved beaches and boardwalks. We couldn't think of a more worthy subject to capture in our art journal. The rides, the saltwater taffy, the blinking lights of the Ferris wheel and the sun-faded pastels of old signage and seaside cottages. All of that and then some.

What's your sweet escape? Where do you go when you just . . . gotta go? Where do your most magical memories live? Take the time to think on this and to gather the elements that will transport you there every time you open your art journal to these stirring pages.

SUPPLIES

Vacation photos

Large Ferris wheel image

Decorative zip-lock plastic bag

Beach sand

Assorted stamps

Black ink pad

Full-page patterned stencil

Assorted patterned paper

Paper ephemera

Faux saltwater taffy stickers

Decorative chipboard accents and letters

Acrylic letters

Canvas paper sheet

Mini bunting banner

Striped treat bags

Black-and-white baker's twine

Enamel color dots

Washi tape

Pink color spray

Assorted Gelatos

Decoupage medium

All-purpose glue

Scissors

#8 round brush

¾"/1.9 cm flat brush

Assorted circular paint spouncers

Gesso

Acrylic paint

* pink
* aqua
* yellow
* black
* gray

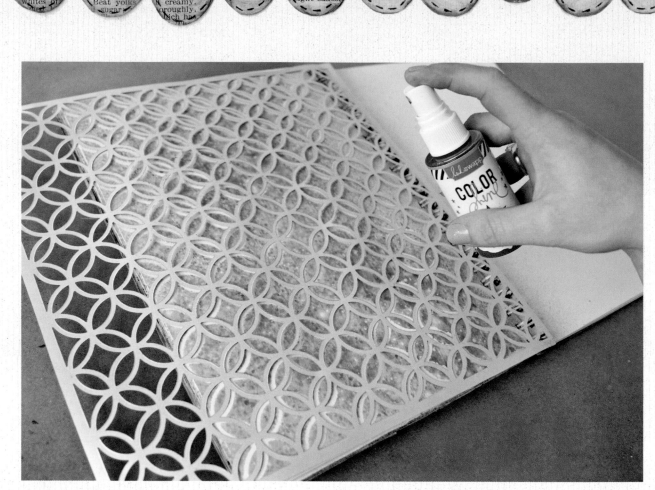

DIRECTIONS

1. Lay your stencil on the page and mist with color spray. Then carefully lift off the stencil and let dry.

2. For two-page spreads like this one, we like when our pages are complementary of each other but composed of completely different elements. So on the page opposite your stenciled page you can make a collage of patterned paper. After you've applied the paper with decoupage medium, let dry for about 5 minutes and seal with decoupage medium.

3. To give the stenciled background a more varied and muted look, apply gesso here and there.

4. With a spouncer paint polka dots for added pops of color.

5. For your first layer of decorative accents, use decoupage medium to adhere whatever your large focal image will be. On the opposing page use pieces of a patterned paper treat bag. Before adhering them, crinkle the paper for added texture.

6. Adhere the crinkled paper pieces and then seal with decoupage medium. Let dry for about 5 minutes.

7. We love to speckle our pages with paint. It's so simple but adds so much to the overall look, especially if you use a few colors. To speckle, combine one part paint with two parts water. Then dip your #8 round brush in this wash, hold the loaded brush above your journal and tap the metal part of your brush to speckle paint upon the page.

8. When your paint speckles are dry to the touch, stamp some images and shapes onto your pages.

9. Distress the edges of your pages with paint. Dip your finger in paint and rub along the edge of the page. It doesn't get easier than that!

10. For extra layering tear pieces of canvas paper in rectangles to fit your words. First cut out the rectangles and then tear away the edges for a worn and distressed look. Tattered canvas fits a beach theme perfectly.

11. Speckle your canvas pieces with paint and apply color to the frayed edges using Gelatos. Working with Gelatos is easy and so rewarding. The colors just glow! Rub the Gelato color onto the frayed edge and then use a wet brush tip to blend and fade the color, giving it a washed-out look.

12. Apply the canvas pieces and letters with all-purpose glue.

13. Add some color to your focal image with Gelatos. Use a wet brush tip to apply the color right from the end of the Gelato.

14. And don't forget to add washi tape accents. (What would we do without washi tape?) We even adhered a packet of actual Jersey Shore sand to our page with a little strip of it.

15. Using all-purpose glue, apply your pileup of decorative accents. Think tickets, tokens, tiny keepsakes and reminders of your travels. For us, the dimensional faux saltwater taffy stickers remind us of our trips down the shore and the treats we always bring home.

16. Add 3-D enamel dot details for dimension, color and texture. And a bunting banner is always festive. Use a bit of baker's twine to string the flags of your banner.

17. Look over your pages and add any final decorative accents. It's done only when you say it's done.

We thought a two-page spread was completely necessary for this theme. It gives you room to do plenty of artful rendering as well as some space for your vacation getaway photos and keepsakes. We love when art journaling meets scrapbooking, and hopefully this will alter the way you look at both of these crafts. A spread like this works great for your favorite holidays too.

WHEN I GROW UP AND HAVE A HOUSE

We've been working artists for *ever*. And still, making art excites us. It's our livelihood AND it's what we do if we have free time. But this persistent urge to create isn't just in the "artist." We think everyone is born with it, only life trains it out of us. Think of how a classroom full of rambunctious kids will become silent once a box of crayons and some paper are introduced. We've all been there. We've all been budding artists at one point.

Well we think an art journal is *the* perfect place to get back to that. Think of those early childhood drawings . . . the house, the tree, the people out front, the sun in the sky. Channel a bit of the budding child artist in you. Get doodle-y. Have some fun with this page but also approach it with all of the experience you've gathered along the way.

SUPPLIES

Heavy gel medium or molding paste

Decoupage medium

All-purpose glue

Stencil

Sharpie marker

Sharpie pen

Watercolor paper

Patterned paper

#4 round brush

#8 round brush

¾"/1.9 cm flat brush

Charcoal pencil

Circular spouncer

Old photograph

Assorted stamps

Scissors

Cake sticker

Gesso

Acrylic paint

* aqua

* pink

* white

* tan

DIRECTIONS

1. Apply a coat of gesso to your page and let dry for 5–10 minutes. Then lay down your stencil in the desired area and apply a thick coat of heavy gel medium or molding paste. You can use a paintbrush or even your finger.

2. Once you've applied a thick coat, lift off your stencil to reveal a dimensional pattern. Let dry thoroughly, at least 10 minutes. A blow dryer will speed up the process. Give it a touch test to make sure it's dry.

3. While the medium or paste dries, draw a simple house shape on watercolor paper and cut patterned paper to fit.

4. Decoupage paper onto your house, apply a topcoat and let dry.

5. Apply gesso over your house paper to mute it a bit and add texture.

6. Draw in the door and window shapes and paint in the white.

7. Sketch in curtains, window frames, roof shingles, etc. Use your small round brush to accent these details. When dry to the touch, use your Sharpie pen to outline everything and add doodle-y accents.

8. When your page is dry, set aside your completed house and add some color to your textured page. With a paintbrush or your fingertip, apply some paint over the textured parts of your page.

9. Add some painted stamps for texture and then collage your page with torn patterned paper. Let dry for about 5–10 minutes and then seal your page with a coat of decoupage medium.

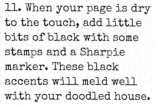

10. Smearing paint is dummy-proof, and it's a great way to add color and varied texture to your collaged background. With a fingertip fade your colors into one another and blend at the seams of your collaged paper. We love the softer look this creates.

11. When your page is dry to the touch, add little bits of black with some stamps and a Sharpie marker. These black accents will meld well with your doodled house.

12. Now it's time to really get things going. First take a look around your page to see where it's lacking color and texture. But keep in mind that you'll be adding lettering. Add some dots of paint with a spouncer, and maybe some paint speckles. We added some pretty roses in a couple of spots that were screaming out for them. Once you've got your embellishments down, cut out your house and people and adhere them to your page with all-purpose glue.

13. We love the smoky, antique-y feel that you get with a charcoal pencil. Lightly trace around your focal images and blend and fade with your fingertip.

14. Adding cut-and-pasted words will make your words bolder than if you were to write them directly onto your background. Write your words on watercolor paper, then cut them out and adhere to your page. We chose a loopy script and filled in the loops with black Sharpie.

15. Now bring it all home with your lettering and any other graphic adornments. Apply your letters with all-purpose glue and maybe add a 3-D image like our cake. (Yes, that's an original Everyday is a Holiday cake sticker!)

After doing this page in our art journal we then pretty much repeated it on a canvas. It's a great image to hang up . . . very "home sweet home." And we hope you got nice and loose with your doodling. That's the whole idea of channeling your childhood drawing techniques. You get to drop your inhibitions about whether it looks good or not—it's simply a house. Are there windows, doors and a roof? Well then, you get an A+!

A Final Note

Upon finishing this book, whether you've completed every single project in full or simply picked up hints and tips from each along the way, the greatest possible outcome is that you're wanting and craving more . . . that you're not yet ready to put away your brushes and palettes or close the cover on your art journal. We hope we've inspired you and that all of those once-hidden talents aren't just out in the open—they're refined. Of course no one becomes an overnight expert at making art. In fact, we may have never even seen an art expert in our lives. And we've been around a ton of artists! Because in art and in living creatively in general, the search never ends. There are always new colors to mix, even if they're just barely a shade brighter than yesterday's paint. So gather your supplies, get out your palette, pour some more paint and make your next masterpiece.

Resources

MICHAELS, WWW.MICHAELS.COM

Acrylic paint

Decoupage medium

Mod Podge

Varnish

Gesso

Golden gel medium

Golden molding paste

Paintbrushes

Watercolor paper

Tracing paper

Art journals

Canvas boards

Canvas paper

Wood plaques

Styrofoam disks

Palette knife

Sharpie pens and markers

All-purpose glue

Texture Crackle by DecoArt

Martha Stewart craft supplies:
* foam circle spouncers
* flocking powder
* combing tool
* faux saltwater taffy 3-D stickers
* 3-D baking theme stickers

Stamps and ink pads

Crayola Air-Dry Clay

StazOn ink pads

E6000 adhesive

Charcoal pencil

Decorative zip-lock plastic bags

DICK BLICK, WWW.DICKBLICK.COM

Paintbrushes

Acrylic paint

Palette knife

Sharpie pens and markers

Canvas boards

Art journals

Watercolor paper

Tracing paper

Decoupage medium

Mod Podge

Varnish

All-purpose glue

Golden gel medium

Gesso

Golden molding paste

Gelatos by Faber Castell

HOME DEPOT, WWW.HOMEDEPOT.COM

DAP acrylic latex caulk

MAYA ROAD,
WWW.MAYAROAD.NET

Color mists

Chipboard accents

Decorative letters and other embellishments

Baker's twine

ELLE'S STUDIO,
WWW.SHOPELLESSTUDIO.COM

Patterned paper

Decorative embellishments

Stamps

HEIDI SWAPP,
WWW.HEIDISWAPP.COM

Patterned paper

Embellishments

Color Shine spritz (pink color spray in
Down the Shore spread)

Down the Shore lettering

Bunting banner

PAM GARRISON,
WWW.PAMGARRISON.TYPEPAD.COM

Stamps (They are some of our favorite stamps that
you'll see on most of our art journal pages.)

MOD PODGE,
WWW.PLAIDONLINE.COM

Mod Podge (For the Sweet Spot Necklace charm,
we used Mod Podgeable Design Elements.)

ETSY, WWW.ETSY.COM

Wooden bracelet (for Your Very Own
Mixed Media Bracelet)

Millinery flowers

Jewelry supplies: ball chain, bails,
jump rings, E6000, wooden beads

Vintage photos

Ephemera

EBAY,
WWW.EBAY.COM

Vintage photos

Vintage trims

Assorted ephemera

Vintage seam binding

TIM HOLTZ,
WWW.TIMHOLTZ.COM

Distress Ink products

SHOP SWEET LULU,
WWW.SHOPSWEETLULU.COM

Striped party straws

Cupcake flags and toppers

Ballerina cake toppers

Striped treat bags

PERSNICKETY PRINTS,
WWW.PERSNICKETYPRINTS.COM

Instagram prints

OCTOBER AFTERNOON,
WWW.OCTOBERAFTERNOON.COM

Patterned paper

Decorative elements

Ferris wheel image (from Down the Shore spread)

BO BUNNY,
WWW.BOBUNNY.COM

Patterned paper

Stamps

Decorative embellishments

RETRO CAFÉ ART,
WWW.RETROCAFEART.COM

Stage curtain collage sheet
(for Fauxbulous Keepsake Cake)

Doll head collage sheet (for the Charlotte
doll on Favorite Things page)

Washi tape

Glass glitter

WWW.SCRAPBOOK.COM

Patterned paper

Stencils

Color sprays

Stamps

Ink pads

Wood veneer shapes and embellishments

Veneer talk bubbles

Enamel color dots

EVERYDAY IS A HOLIDAY,
WWW.EVERYDAYISAHOLIDAY.
BIGCARTEL.COM

Sticker sheets

Patterned paper

Cake and cupcake images

Template (resize to fit your canvas)

Acknowledgments

We'd very humbly like to acknowledge the generous and talented people who've directly or indirectly contributed to the making of this book:

Our publisher, Will Kiester, for having such amazing knowledge and foresight as to what this book could and should be, and for trusting us, respecting us and being able to see the makings of a great book in probably just a few glimpses at our *oeuvre*, and over the course of one very excited conference call.

Our editor, Marissa Giambelluca, for being very patient, affable, intuitive and sharp—trust us, those are rare and special qualities—and for making the writing of this book as easy as possible for us.

Also to Meg Palmer at Page Street for all of her super-valuable assistance and input along the way.

Natalie Slater, author of *Bake and Destroy*, and certified all-around cool gal. May everyone in the world know, love and envy the wit and wisdom of this tattooed Wonder Woman.

Over the years we've become friends with some fabulous women who keep our beloved creative community alive. They sacrifice so much of their time and energy for fellow artists and lovers of art, all in the name of art and friendship—and not particularly in that order. They are:

Ellen Legare and Sallianne McClelland of Art Is . . . You

Kim Caldwell of Artistic Affaire

Teresa McFayden of Silver Bella

Jo Packham of The Creative Connection

Lisa Kettell of Art Opera

Rosalyn-Sue Smith and Jennifer Hayslip of Sweethearts on the Homefront

And these pillars of our creative community:

Cathie Filian, Emmy-nominated host of *Creative Juice* on HGTV, producer of *Craft Wars* on TLC and best-selling author

Kathy Cano-Murillo, CraftyChica.com

Matthew Mead, founder, creative director and editor-in-chief of *Holiday with Matthew Mead Magazine* series

Cheryl and Griffith Day, authors of *The Back in the Day Bakery Cookbook*

Jane Dagmi, *HGTV Remodels*, *Designing Spaces*

Jacqueline deMontravel, *Romantic Homes*

Claudine Hellmuth, nationally recognized collage artist, author and illustrator

About the Authors

Jenny Heid (aka Jenny Holiday) and Aaron Nieradka have been living the artful life together for nearly two decades and specialize in everything from restoring antique furniture, to painting murals, to having a retail shop, to creating hand-painted furniture and a home decor collection. Their designs have been sold at top retailers such as Michaels, Barnes & Noble, Paper Source and in boutiques and shops worldwide. They're the designers behind the ubiquitous Keep Calm and Have a Cupcake line of stationery and gifts available everywhere. Their artwork has graced the pages of magazines such as *Country Living*, *Country Home*, *Woman's Day Decorating Ideas*, *Design New Jersey*, *Romantic Homes*, *Somerset Life*, *Somerset Studio*, *Where Women Cook* and *The New York Times Magazine*. Their work has also been featured on NBC's *Today Show* with Matt Lauer.

They've been instructors at many national venues including Silver Bella in Omaha, Nebraska; The Creative Connection in St. Paul, Minnesota; Art Opera in Red Bank, New Jersey; Art Is . . . You in Stamford, Connecticut; and Artistic Affaire in Los Angeles, California.

Jenny and Aaron can currently be found on their blog, Everyday is a Holiday, sharing their creative process, latest obsessions, newest paintings and designs, some of their favorite recipes and tales of living the creative life together, along with their two Chihuahuas, on the Jersey Shore.

Index